# Sunshine

## by Gail Saunders-Smith

Content Consultant:
Ken Barlow, Chief Meteorologist
KARE-TV, Minneapolis
Member, American Meteorological Society

## Pebble Books
an imprint of Capstone Press

# Pebble Books

Pebble Books are published by Capstone Press
818 North Willow Street, Mankato, Minnesota 56001
http://www.capstone-press.com

*Library of Congress Cataloging-in-Publication Data*
Saunders-Smith, Gail.
    Sunshine/by Gail Saunders-Smith.
        p. cm.
    Includes bibliographical references and index.
    Summary: Describes the effects of light from the sun on earth and how it causes temperature
changes, the seasons, winds, and clouds.
    ISBN 1-56065-780-4
    1. Sunshine—Juvenile literature.  2. Weather—Juvenile literature.
[1. Sunshine.]  I. Title.
    QC911.2.S28 1998
    551.5'271—dc21                          98-5045
                                          CIP
                                          AC

## Note to Parents and Teachers

This book describes and illustrates how sunshine affects the weather on earth. The close picture-text matches support early readers in understanding the text. The text offers subtle challenges with compound and complex sentence structures. This book also introduces early readers to expository and content-specific vocabulary. The expository vocabulary is defined in the Words to Know section. Early readers may need assistance in reading some of these words. Readers also may need assistance in using the Table of Contents, Words to Know, Read More, Internet Sites, and Index/Word List sections of the book.

# Table of Contents

Sunshine is light from the sun. Sunshine gives the earth light and heat. Sunshine also makes weather on the earth.

Light from the sun travels to the earth in rays. The rays heat the atmosphere. Atmosphere is the air around the earth.

Sunshine falls on one-half of the earth at a time. It is day on one side of the earth. It is night on the other side. The earth spins. It moves places into and out of the light.

The equator is halfway between the top and the bottom of the earth. Sunshine is strongest at places near the equator. At noon, the sun is straight up in the sky. Sunshine makes the air very hot at the equator.

Photo: Galapagos Island, Ecuador

Sunshine is weaker at places near the top and bottom of the earth. The sun does not go up very high in the sky. Sunshine does not heat the air as much. These places have ice and snow all year long.

Photo: Antarctica

Sunshine makes the seasons on the earth. In June, the top of earth points toward the sun. More sunshine hits the top half of the earth. It is summer here. Less sunshine hits the bottom half of the earth. It is winter there.

In December, the top of the earth points away from the sun. Less sunshine hits the top half of the earth. It is winter here. More sunshine hits the bottom half of the earth. It is summer there.

18

Sunshine heats the atmosphere. The rays of the sun heat some places more than others. This causes pockets of colder air and pockets of warmer air. These air pockets move and make wind.

Sunshine also heats bodies of water on the earth. The water evaporates. Evaporate means to go into the air. The water in the air gathers into clouds. The clouds carry water around the earth.

# Words to Know

*atmosphere*—the air around the earth

*equator*—places that are halfway between the top and the bottom of earth are on the equator

*evaporate*—when something wet goes into the air; when water evaporates, it turns into vapor

*season*—one of the four parts of a year; spring, summer, autumn, and winter

*weak*—not strong

# Read More

Fowler, Allan. *Energy from the Sun.* New York: Children's Press, 1997.

Grazzini, Francesca. *Sun, Where Do You Go?* Brooklyn, N.Y.: Kane/Miller Book Publishers, 1996.

Palmer, Joy. *Sunshine.* Austin, Tex.: Raintree Steck-Vaughn Publishers, 1993.

Vogt, Gregory L. *The Sun.* Brookfield, Conn.: Millbrook Press, 1996.

# Internet Sites

A Virtual Tour of the Sun
http://www.astro.uva.nl/michielb/od95

Our Sun
http://observe.ivv.nasa.gov/nasa/exhibits.sun/sunframe.html

Stanford SOLAR Center
http://solar-center.stanford.edu

# Index/Word List

**Word Count: 307**
**Early-Intervention Level: 14**

**Editorial Credits**
Lois Wallentine, editor; Timothy Halldin, design; Michelle L. Norstad, photo research

**Photo Credits**
William B. Folsom, 18
International Stock/Ronn Maratea, 12
William Munoz, 8
Photo Network International/Nancy Hoyt Belcher, 10
Chuck Place, 1, 4
Cheryl R. Richter, 6
Richard Hamilton Smith, cover, 14, 20
Unicorn Stock Photos/Jeff Greenberg, 16